Rules & Procedures

For Character Education

The First Step Toward School Civility

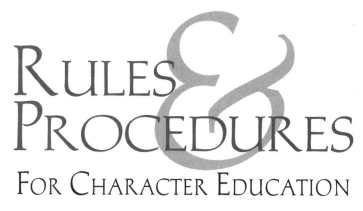

2ND EDITION

BY
DR. PHILIP FITCH VINCENT

RULES & PROCEDURES

FOR CHARACTER EDUCATION

THE FIRST STEP TOWARD SCHOOL CIVILITY

2nd Edition

by Dr. Philip Fitch Vincent

Produced and published by
CHARACTER DEVELOPMENT GROUP

Phone (919) 967–2110,   (919) 967–2139 fax

E-mail: respect96@aol.com

www.CharacterEducation.com

Cover design by Paul Turley

Book design by Sandy Nordman Design

Text editing by Ginny Turner

ISBN 0-892056-06-2 $10.00

CHAPTER
Contents

"What the best and wisest parent wants for his own child, that must the community want for all of its children. Any other ideal for our schools is narrow and unlovely, acted upon, it destroys our democracy."

John Dewey, *School and Society*, 1910

Acknowledgements

RULES AND PROCEDURES: The First Step Toward School Civility is the first book in a five-book series utilizing the "hub and spokes" of character education. Rules and procedures are at the hub and are critical to the implementation of the four spokes of character education, and so were the subject of the first book. The spokes will be featured in books over the next several years. Each of these books will be written by experts in their field and will provide background and insights in assisting schools and school districts to develop solid approaches to character education. I look forward to continuing dialogue with these authors as I work to enhance my own understanding of solid character education practices.

This book would not have been possible without the insights of individuals such as Kevin Ryan, Tom Lickona, Henry Huffman and William Damon. The clarity of your writing illuminates difficult issues and forces us, who aspire to write a few words, to be clear and concise in our attempts. Although I will credit you when I am successful, I will not hold you responsible for my failures.

I am particularly grateful for my friendship with David Wangaard from the School for Ethical Education in Bridgeport, Connecticut. David's insights in this text cannot be overestimated. The hours we have spent in discussions have greatly enhanced my knowledge of character education and, more importantly, have contributed to a friendship which continues to grow.

I am grateful for the fresh ideas of practitioners around the country. Whether I am working in North Carolina, Texas, Oregon, Connecticut, or any of my other destinations, excellent educators challenge me in my assumptions and force me to think and re-think my assertions. You teach me far more than I ever teach you.

Thanks to Dixon Smith, Lisa Brumback, and editor Ginny Turner at Character Development Group. They assist countless people around the country in their character education efforts.

Finally, I thank my wife, Cynthia, and daughter, Mary Kathryn. I am only able to continue to travel because of your support and constant love.

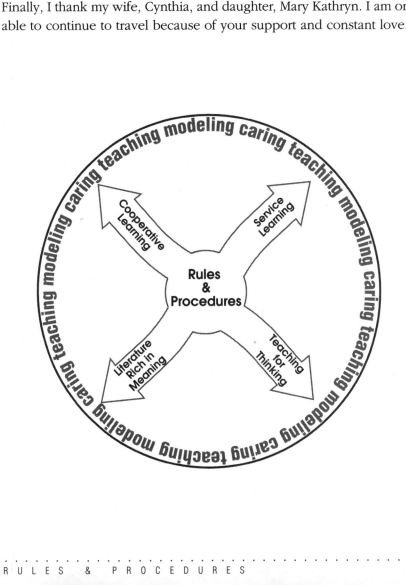

Introduction

The core problem facing our schools is a moral one. All the other problems derive from it. Hence, all the various attempts at school reform are unlikely to succeed unless character education is put at the top of the agenda. If students don't learn self discipline and respect for others, they will continue to exploit each other sexually no matter how many health clinics and condom distribution plans are created. If they don't learn habits of courage and justice, curriculums designed to improve their self-esteem won't stop the epidemic of extortion, bullying, and violence; neither will courses designed to make them more sensitive to diversity....If they don't acquire intellectual virtues such as commitment to learning, objectivity, respect for the truth, and humility in the face of facts, then critical-thinking strategies will only amount to one more gimmick in the curriculum.

William Kilpatrick
Why Johnny Can't Tell Right From Wrong

William Kilpatrick's analysis of school reform needing character education at the top of its agenda has never been more relevant as we approach the twenty-first century. This moral problem facing our schools he alludes to is one that has recuperative potential. Remedying this problem calls for the provision of a moral environment in schools for all students. Such an environment requires structure bounded by fairness. This environment emphasizes a love of learning balanced with a love of good action, which leads to civility. James Kauffman and Harold Burbach (1997) recognize the importance of basic civilities:

> At a minimum, the kind of social climate we envision is one in which everyone, teachers and students alike, treats others with consideration and respect and in which mannerly behavior and small courtesies are the norm. More optimistically, we believe that a classroom where civility holds sway is one that is well on its way to facilitating classroom cooperation, responsible self-governance, and democratic living. (p. 322)

This type of environment prompts a school to operate as a good community, thus enabling students to function within the dynamics of a good community. But it is not enough merely to prompt students. Educators must recognize the importance of modeling good habits so students can develop such behaviors themselves. If we insist that students be fair and honest, we must be fair and honest. If we desire that students be caring, we must be caring. If we want students to be polite, we must be polite. Remember, most character is not taught—it is caught!

Modeling is necessary, but it alone is not enough to insure that a moral climate exists in a school. Students need time to work together, to reflect and discuss ideas that are the natural result of good readings, and to serve others in the school and community. But as a prerequisite to all curriculum presentations, students need order and structure. Developing guidelines through rules and procedures helps insure order and structure and therefore a good and just community.

It is elementary that good parents and teachers spend time on establishing such productive rules and procedures. Children exposed to these helpful guidelines, which nurture habits of respect, responsibility, perseverance, and similar traits are more likely to be successful in school and in life than those who are unexposed.

As we examine *rules* and *procedures* and construct a corroborative platform on which to begin our discussion, let us define these terms in a workable context.

The *New World Dictionary of the American Language* defines **rule** as: *an authoritative regulation for action, conduct, method, procedure, arrangement, etc. [the rules of the school].* **Procedure** is defined as: *the act, method, or manner of proceeding in some process or course of action; esp., the sequence of steps to be followed. 2. a particular course of action or way of doing something.*

We can infer, then, that rules set the standard that conduct tries to meet. Procedures tell us what to do to meet the objectives of the rule(s). The practice of procedures leads to a following of the rules and the subsequent development of good habits of action. Developing good character traits, as Aristotle has noted, is habitual. The failure to cultivate good habits such as respect, punctuality, courtesy, and responsibility dooms a child to actions based on impulses, without the character needed to develop into a good citizen.

Luckily, the majority of students recognizes the importance of observing rules and procedures. Indeed, without an understanding of basic rules and procedures, behavior results that is counterproductive to positive living and learning.

However, there is ample evidence that far too many students today are rejecting following rules and practicing appropriate procedures. Many are favoring actions based on their individual desires without regard to the potential outcomes. We need only talk with educators to learn that the overall behavior of students in schools has seriously deteriorated from even 20 years ago. In general, students are exhibiting less respect for teachers and for their peers. They are more prone to break or disregard rules and accepted norms of behavior at school and within the community.

The Josephson Institute's 1996 study of 6,000 high school students noted that 87 percent of them believed that, on a practical basis, honesty is the best policy. (One can only wonder what the other 13 percent believe!)

Based on other responses within the survey, however, it is clear this statement concerning the importance of honesty is not carrying over to other behaviors.

- Two-thirds of the students (65 percent) admitted they had cheated on an exam in the previous year and about half, or 47 percent, said they had done so more than once.
- Forty-two percent of high school male respondents and 31 percent of high school females said they had stolen something from a store within the previous 12 months.
- More than half the high school male respondents (55 percent) and one-third of the females (36 percent) said it is sometimes justified to respond to an insult or verbal abuse with physical force.

Very similar results came out of their 1998 study on the same issues.

William Bennett, in *The Index of Leading Cultural Indicators: Facts and Figures on the State of American Society* (1994), noted some chilling trends of students in or near schools.

- About 3 million thefts and violent crimes occur on or near a school campus each year, representing nearly 16,000 incidents per day.
- Twenty percent of high school students now carry a firearm, knife, razor, club, or some other weapon on a regular basis.

These statistics raise the all-important question: *Why is this occurring?* Children can't be totally accountable for these trends. They have learned these behaviors from someone; they aren't born with such negative tendencies. To put it bluntly, they have learned these actions from adults. We are in charge of raising the next generation. Our lack of consistency and proper instruction and modeling has created a climate where standards have not been taught and reinforced. Children are born with certain dispositions that can be developed into moral behavior (more about this will follow in Chapter 2). However, if they are left without a guide— without a moral compass—they may choose a more harmful and potentially destructive path. Children, for the most part, act based on what is expected of them. They learn by observation and by instruction. They learn by the development of good and bad habits.

Despite the preceding statistics, the majority of our students have been taught to be civil and caring toward others and practice this most of the time. They are on the path to good citizenship. However, simply striving for a majority is not adequate. All of our students deserve the opportunity to develop good habits to assist them throughout their lives. In helping them develop their character—to *know the good, love the good and do the good*—we as parents and educators are giving them tools to navigate through their lives. This book will focus on how rules and procedures can facilitate this process.

RULES & PROCEDURES

1

RULES AND PROCEDURES GENERATE A WINNING CLIMATE IN SCHOOLS

Life is regulated by rules and procedures. Think of all the rules just in the area of vehicles: We must register our cars and pay for a license plate, we must take a driving test to get an operator's license, we must obey the rules of the road, we must stop when a policeman's vehicle comes up behind us and signals us to stop. We might complain about all the trouble, but if it weren't for those rules, we'd have chaos on our streets and highways, and it wouldn't be safe for anyone to drive anywhere. Rules bring order to our activities, allow other people to predict how we'll probably behave, offer some threat of consequences for not following them, and enable us to feel safe enough to drive with our loved ones anywhere in the country. Rules connect and protect the community. They are the expectations for appropriate behavior. Procedures make the expectations a reality. They are the practices or the acts that one performs that show understanding of the expectations.

A college student who wants to graduate agrees to follow the rules about required class hours for graduation, and follows the procedures for registering or dropping classes. This insures that all students who receive degrees have met the requirements, and the value of the degree is not degraded. Rules covering behavior on college campuses include returning or compensating for all library books before graduation, and prohibition of alcohol in campus buildings. These rules insure protection of the college's resources and encourage a civil climate for all students.

Likewise, if public and private schools want to have a civil climate for students, teachers, and staff, they need to have rules that establish how students should act. Following rules that help create discipline and good habits helps create a civil environment within which teachers and students can operate. The procedures are how we act. They are the practices that allow us to model being respectful, responsible, and caring. Without the procedures, the expectations are just that—expectations. They are not actions. Simply put, it rules and procedures create civility by which the process of education—an education of inspiration and reflection—can grow.

Good habits and character development are founded on obeying rules and practices. Any longtime teacher will tell you that the failure of students to develop respectful social habits and to follow rules and procedures can handicap them in developing their intellectual skills. And any company personnel director will tell you that failure of employees to follow rules and procedures will handicap their success in any career.

As the school climate of caring and civility grows, a safe and orderly environment should evolve, and academic achievement will rise. If a school lacks a positive climate, both intellectual and character development will face difficulty. This shouldn't surprise us. As adults, we like schedules and structure, especially within our work environment. It helps us do our work better when we know basically what to expect through the day and generally how those around us will act. Why should we desire anything less for our children? To establish a safe and orderly environment, we must first determine the characteristics that will guide us in the formation of the environment.

In nurturing self-disciplined children, we need to establish boundaries and solid structures from which they might produce virtuous behaviors. Emile Durkheim, the esteemed 19th-century sociologist, reminds us that "...solely by imposing limits can a child be liberated." Similarly, by imposing limits in schools through the generation of rules and procedures, students will cultivate the habits needed as prerequisites for becoming good students and citizens.

The issue of punctuality offers an illustration of why having a tardy rule for students and teachers encourages timely attendance. Many will comply because they recognize that, if people are habitually late, no serious instruction can occur. Others will follow the tardy rule because of the potential consequences that result from being tardy to class. Although we may follow the rules based on consequences, we can, through practice, develop the habit of punctuality and a sense of responsibility and commitment to ourselves and others.

Aristotle suggests this in the *Nicomachean Ethics* in which he describes two kinds of virtue. He delineates intellectual virtue as the contemplative side of virtue that is experienced through thinking and reflecting over ideas. Learning to think clearly and applying logic to ethical issues help enhance intellectual virtue.

Aristotle's second type of virtue, and the type this short work will consider, is moral virtue. This virtue is sustained through the formulation and practice of good habits. This would include, but is not limited to, being punctual, respectful, courageous, responsible, and caring. By instilling these moral virtues or good habits in students, we are instituting rules that should be considered expectations of appropriate behavior leading to good citizenship. The procedures are the practices needed to establish the habits of good citizenship.

> VIRTUES—The character traits we should strive to develop in students.
> RULES—The expectations designed for appropriate student behavior.
> PROCEDURES—The practices needed to develop the habits of following rules and developing good character.

Consider the following example:
> **Virtue** = Respect
> **Rule** = Treat all people with respect.
> **Procedures** = Do not interrupt others when they are speaking. Practice active listening. Use polite language, such as please and thank you, to everyone.

Another way of looking at this linkage is provided by Dr. David Wangaard from the School for Ethical Education in Bridgeport, Connecticut. Wangaard arrives at the importance of rules and procedures by having teachers or students state the expectations of appropriate behavior. He then asks individuals to state what this behavior looks like. "How would I know when students and teachers are acting with respect? What would I see occurring in the environment?" After this is determined, one can easily state the rule: Treat all people with respect.

Consider the following example:

Expectations: Students will model respectful behavior.

Procedures: Students will be polite to others (e.g., saying please, thank you, excuse me). Students will practice active listening.

Rules: Treat all people with respect.

Both of these processes can help achieve the climate that students and teachers deserve. Educators yearn to work in a civil, nurturing climate where the students are so respectful and self-disciplined teachers can delight in the process of teaching. A school's climate determines the success it will have, if any, in germinating respect, self-discipline and other character traits in its students. Unfortunately, many schools don't have a caring, nurturing climate and the teachers and staff are faced with the challenge of creating one from a quite different environment. How does one begin?

THE IMPORTANCE OF CLIMATE IN CHARACTER BUILDING

James Leming presents in a nutshell the connection between school climate and rules and procedures. In an article entitled "In Search of Effective Character Education," he writes:

> Character develops within a social web or environment. The nature of that environment, the messages it sends to individuals, and the behaviors it encourages and discourages, are important factors to consider in character education. Clear rules of conduct, student ownership of those rules, a supportive environment and satisfaction resulting from complying with the norms of the environment shape behavior. (p. 69)

How can we tell what our school climate is? Certainly each employee of a school has a good idea based on his or her own subjective experience, but it's important and more accurate to get a bigger picture. Talk to key people at the school who are not limited to the view from one classroom. A central office supervisor is a great contact for names of teachers who travel between schools, perhaps as teachers of English as a second language, foreign language, art, music, or other subjects. Such personnel have a broader, less emotional view of a school. Similarly, an experienced substitute teacher who works at several schools could tell you in an instant which schools she prefers to work at, and why. It's worthwhile to ask any or all people like these to describe your school's climate. Particular areas of interest:

1. Attentiveness of students
2. Observed parental involvement
3. Working relationships with other staff
4. Evidence of politeness and civility between all in the building

The school secretary/registrar can provide data about student attendance, discipline referrals, and teacher absences. The numbers of absences and referrals are indicators of the degree of supportiveness existing in the school's environment. When the climate is nurturing, educators perform better and students learn more. Teacher absences might be affected by special circumstances, such as a serious illness or pregnancy, but in general, a high number of absences on Monday and Friday is a signal flag of low morale or burnout.

Teachers of electives, such as physical education, music, art, or vocational education, can reveal the nature of students' manners when they come to class. These teachers can answer questions like: Are the students orderly when they arrive and leave as a group? Respectful of the teacher who brings them and of each other when they work in class? Caring toward other students' feelings about their work? Do they follow schools rules and procedures? Or, are the electives teachers continually having to call for order and to discipline students? Custodians and cafeteria personnel can tell you a lot about a school's climate that the principal might not see or hear.

The climate of a school is a clear reflection of its inhabitants. Generally, a school with an inviting climate has educators and students who enjoy being at school. Schools with good climates have people who want to build relationships with each other. Dr. Jim Sweeney, a nationally recognized expert in fostering a positive school climate, notes in *Tips for Improving School Climate*:

> Climate is a term used to describe how people feel about their school. It is a combination of beliefs, values, and attitudes shared by students, teachers, administrators, parents, bus drivers, office personnel, custodians, cafeteria workers, and others who play an important role in the life of the school. When a school has a "winning climate," people feel proud, connected, and committed. They support, help and care for each other. When the climate is right, there is a certain joy in coming to school, either to teach or to learn. (p.1)

Suppose you work in a school similar to the school Dr. Sweeney describes. How would you describe the learning activities of the students in this winning climate? We might hypothesize that the students are involved in their learning, that they are enthusiastic knowledge seekers and exercise their natural curiosities to explore and reflect on their environment. In this climate, students strive to go "above and beyond" minimal academic standards and to develop character traits, such as respect and responsibility, which they will use throughout their lives.

Educators aid in this process through modeling appropriate social behavior with the understanding that not all good character is taught, more is caught through observation of others. Educators plant seeds in students, which will bear the fruit of good behavior. For some students, modeling of good behavior and the statement of the rules are enough to engender persistent good habits. Other students want to see what will happen when they don't follow certain rules and must be shown the consequences for their actions (more about this in Chapter 4). A good school helps young people grow into good citizens through instruction, modeling, and an insistence on following rules for the betterment of everyone in the school.

When a school has a good climate, people interact warmly and positively, and a strong sense of community develops. This is what all educators and students deserve. To achieve this climate, a school must have rules and procedures that are followed and supported by both teachers and students. A good climate is the fertile soil in which Aristotle's moral virtues sprout, grow, and bloom. Consider the following scenarios regarding rules and procedures and their impact on school climate.

Scenario 1

A high school principal, Ms. Elton, became very concerned about the noise and disturbances that were taking place in the halls during class changes. Somehow, general activity and conversation had gradually escalated into raucous, physical melee seven times a day. Several students had been pushed down accidentally and stepped on. One suffered a broken arm. The school had rules and procedures governing how students were to behave, but it was clear students were not following the rules— or enough of them weren't that the entire student body was endangered. The principal called on another principal, Ms. Reese, to help analyze this problem.

The two principals stood in the halls at different places during a class change that was, as usual, extremely loud and disruptive. After the class change, the two returned to the principal's office. Ms. Reese asked to see the rules and procedures of the school, which included rules on how students were to act during class changes, and what teachers were to be doing.

Ms. Reese pointed out that the teachers were not standing in the hall during the class changes, as the school rules called for. They were supposed to be there to promote civil dialogue and model caring towards the students. The hall had ten classrooms, but not one teacher was standing in the hall during the class changes.

Ms. Elton called a staff meeting, in which everyone expressed great concern about the noise and potential for disturbances in the hall. She reviewed the rules and procedures of the school and asked how many teachers had been standing in the hall. Few hands appeared. She reminded them that the reason for being in the hall—the reason the rule had been established—was to help instill a sense of civility in the students by modeling caring and civil behavior. She reminded them that when students observe civil, caring behavior, students will begin to model civil dialogue and caring behavior toward their peers and teachers. The teachers agreed to return to the hall during class changes.

In the meantime, Ms. Elton directed leaders of the student government to address this issue with their homeroom representatives, who would review with all students the existing rules and procedures for proper behavior in the hall. Within a short period of time the students were a bit quieter during the class change, and grew more so when teachers standing outside their classrooms reminded them to keep their voices down and to walk with consideration for others. Students and teachers began exchanging greetings and small talk during the class changes, strengthening their own relationships and modeling civil behavior for other students. Together they were improving the climate of the school by following their rules and procedures. Through practice, habits of good behavior were being developed.

Scenario 2

An elementary school was having problems with its after-school bus students. A guidance counselor, Ms. Bolton, noticed that, on some days, the students came into the cafeteria and began schoolwork while they waited for their bus. On other days, they came into the cafeteria, never got started on their work and grew were loud and disruptive.

After a week of study, Ms. Bolton discovered that the staff teacher on bus duty determined how the students acted. The counselor knew this should not occur because there were clear rules and procedures about how students were to act upon arriving in the cafeteria. Ms. Bolton kept records about after-school behavior each day and who was in charge, which she shared with the principal and the Building Leadership Team (BLT). The BLT decided to place this concern on the faculty meeting agenda. At that meeting the principal reviewed the rules and procedures *teachers and students* should follow upon entering the cafeteria, as well as how to deal with students when they choose not to follow the rules.

The teachers and teacher assistants agreed that, to help the students learn the habit of doing their schoolwork while waiting for the late bus, they must be consistent with their expectation and enforcement of the procedures. The teachers reviewed the procedures again with the students. To develop responsibility in completing all homework, each student was to come into the cafeteria and work on homework without talking for 20 minutes. After that time, the staff would allow quiet talking. Because the rules and procedures were made clear to the students, and because all supervising teachers were enforcing procedures, in a short period of time, all the students were using the wait to work on their homework. A better climate was created in the school through consistency with the rules and following the procedures.

Note what these two scenarios have in common: Both had existing rules and procedures to govern how the students and teachers were supposed to act. The educators and students knew the rules and procedures, yet they had become slack in their practice, allowing deterioration of climate in their schools. They had stopped acting with the total community in mind.

Perhaps these scenarios seem too simple. After all, excessive noise in the hall or in the after-school-care waiting area may not be a major issue to some people. But don't underestimate the effect of the contradictory message to students. A school decides it will allow teachers to determine whether students are tardy to class. One week later, disorder is rampant in the halls. Some teachers require that students be in their seats when the tardy bell rings. Others let students in the room and don't count them tardy until five minutes after the tardy bell rings. What are the students learning? They learn that being punctual depends on who is judging. Punctuality is relative. Punctuality can be five minutes late. Is this what we want students to learn? Is this a habit we want them to develop? Is this a way to teach or model a virtue? Is this a way to build consensus? Is this the way to run a school? Expecting students to be civil in the entire school environment is a reasonable expectation. Excessive noise may seem like a small problem, but it diminishes the efforts toward creating good habits—and therefore good character.

Rules (the standards) and *procedures* (actions practiced and habits instilled to reach the standards) are essential for the smooth functioning of a school, but they will only be effective if they are consistently expected and practiced. We all value consistency; otherwise life is chaotic and unproductive. Thirteen-year-old Jimmy, wrote a letter to his father, which was published on Father's Day in Ann Landers' column, June 15, 1997. In it, he expresses gratitude for his parents' consistent rules:

> "I like the way you don't let me get away with much. Sometimes I act mad when I don't get my way, but deep down I am glad you are strict. I would be scared to death if you let me do anything I want. I like that you and Mom agree on the rules around here. At Tommy's house, if his mom says he can't do something, he goes and asks his dad because he knows his dad will say OK just to get rid of him."

To develop the habits of good behavior that Jimmy writes about, we must be consistent with what we model and in what we expect. In Ken Beck and Jim Clark's *The Andy Griffith Show Book* (1985), Opie Taylor, Sheriff Andy Taylor's son in the popular 1960s television series, is a benefactor of consistent rules and modeling. Beck and Clark write:

> The younger Taylor knows exactly what his father expects of him, whether it be chores around the house or at the courthouse, or his conduct in the classroom or on the playground. Andy has taught Opie the importance of responsibility, respect and honesty.

If students are to develop the skills needed to be good students and good citizens, we as parents and educators need to determine practices that will enhance learning, set limits, be consistent with enforcement, and model the behavior we expect. The development of character in students is a slow, cumulative process, and we can aid most by showing them where we want them to go, and directing and reinforcing the practices needed to get there.

The next section focuses on the logistics needed to help foster good habits in students which can be accomplished through the establishment, practice, and following of rules and procedures.

REVIEW

1 Life is regulated by rules and procedures.

2 According to Aristotle, there are two types of virtue—*intellectual*, which develops the contemplative side of virtue, and *moral*, which is sustained and developed by the formulation and practice of good habits and/or virtues.

3 We must determine the virtues or good habits we wish to develop in ourselves and in students (e.g., respect, responsibility) and formulate the habits or practices which, if practiced, will contribute to the development of that virtue.

4 We must consistently model and practice the virtues we wish our students to adopt.

RULES & PROCEDURES

2

CLEAR RULES OF CONDUCT SHAPE POSITIVE STUDENT BEHAVIOR

Years ago, I participated in a conference between a parent of a primary grade student and several educators. The child was highly undisciplined and causing much concern within the classroom. During one of the discussions, I asked the mother to explain her home discipline policy. She replied that she didn't discipline her child much, for fear it would stifle his creativity. I asked her to name any highly creative person who had not been disciplined. She was surprised by my question and the light began to dawn for her that disciplining her child might actually help him.

As the discussion progressed, we agreed that setting and enforcing limits in the home for appropriate behavior can enhance a child's creativity by establishing comfortable parameters for him to function within. We also discussed how parameters aid in restoring order and providing a harmonious environment. By the end of the conference, the mother left with a new understanding of the value of discipline and some clear ideas of how to set limits and consequences for her child's unruly behavior.

Within a couple weeks, the boy's teacher noted a significant improvement in his classroom behavior and his ability to take direction. And as time went on, he continued to improve. His grades went up, and he was allowed more time in class to work on the creative activities he most enjoyed. About two months after our initial meeting, the mother sent a note to those of us who had been there that she was doing a better job at home sticking to her new rules and helping her son set up procedures regarding appropriate behavior. Though he definitely didn't like her new system when she launched it, she said she was consistent in holding her son accountable for failing to follow directions or meet expectations. The boy's teacher augmented this work by further reinforcing his emerging self-control in the classroom. Everyone—parent, teacher, and boy—were happier about the situation.

Being disciplined and able to follow rules, learned through the practice of procedures, is desirable for all children. We cannot empower children to think and act properly unless the children understand the rules and have developed good habits (learn and practice good procedures). Fortunately, we are programmed at birth to grow and develop good habits of caring and concern. William Damon in his work, *Greater Expectations* (1995) writes:

> The seeds of the moral sense are sown at conception, and its roots are firmly established at birth. Every infant enters this world prepared to respond socially, and in a moral manner, to others. Every child has the capacity to acquire moral character. The necessary emotional response systems, budding cognitive awareness, and personal dispositions are there from the start. Although, unfortunately, not every child grows into a responsible and caring person, the potential to do so is native to every member of the species. (p. 132)

Damon's premise is that the wiring is in place in children for the development of good moral citizens before they are born. Children from a very early age are constantly observing their world, seeking to understand the process and order in it. They want to find fairness and goodness, first for themselves and then as they get older, for others, too. With their quick aptitude for learning and natural openness, they can very willingly adopt the attitudes and practices that yield highly moral individuals. Yet merely having the wiring doesn't guarantee that a child will develop into a good citizen. Having the capability does not guarantee development of moral character.

Damon argues that there are four overlapping processes present and active at birth:
- Moral emotions, such as empathy, fear and guilt
- Moral judgment to determine conduct in matters of justice, care, truthfulness, responsibility, and ethical duty

- Social cognition to relate to the social world
- Self-understanding to glean awareness of our past, present, and future self and to master self-control.

To round out the development of a good, caring, and civil person, we must add instruction, modeling, and practice. This requires caring adults and a consistent environment that seeks to develop respectful, responsible children and students. If you want children to be honest, you as a parent or teacher have to be honest. A woman once told me, "I found a hundred-dollar bill just outside a restaurant, but my daughter was with me, so I had to turn it in." Do we want to say that we turned it in because our child was with us, or just that we found the bill and turned it in? What was fortunate was that her daughter was with her so it became a teachable moment. Through education and modeling in family life, we socialize children to become adults. It's not hard to make an impression because they look up to us and want to be like us. Even when they seem not to notice, they are paying very close attention to our words and actions. Sometimes they point out the smallest inconsistencies between what we say to do and what we actually do. Who hasn't had that happen?

The truth can cause a parent or teacher much chagrin at times. When my daughter was three years old, she and I were riding in a car near our home. A car pulled out in front of us, which I narrowly missed. Without thinking, I blurted out a choice line of words. Several weeks later we had another near–accident. I didn't need to say the words; my daughter did! She modeled perfectly what she had heard, both the phrasing and the application.

However, not everyone believes that we should "socialize" children by modeling appropriate behavior. The 18th-century French philosopher Jean-Jacques Rousseau maintained that children should be children before they become adults. He believed that children have their own unique ways of thinking and feeling. Common sense tells us this. However, his approach to child rearing, described in great detail in his work *Emile* states that children should not be contaminated by the world. He maintained that, left to their own accord, they will develop into morally sensitive individuals through their intuitions, experiences, and feelings. Of course there is no evidence to support this. Rousseau may have correctly gleaned that children have the seeds of morality in them, but he failed to recognize the importance that interactions with caring adults of good character play in the development of the good child.

Daniel Goleman, in his book *Emotional Intelligence* (1995), reported that two-year-old children who have been raised in nurturing homes will try to comfort a friend who is crying. Children who have been abused or neglected early in their life tend to yell at or hit crying children. Without a range of positive experiences from nurturing parents, the neglected children had no compassionate or comforting skills to call upon.

Even with the types of incidents like these, supporters of the laissez-faire child-rearing theory have gained steam by stretching the work of Jean Piaget's educational development concept into the so-called "child–centered" classroom. William Damon recognized this distortion of Piaget's work when he states that, in educational terminology, child centered "…generally means a laissez-faire approach that allows children to proceed at their own pace, pursue their own interests, and learn from their own actions. It follows from what is known as a 'constructivist' perspective on learning—a position also widely attributed to Piaget." (p. 102)

Piaget believed that children construct their own learning and meaning from the world, but that doesn't mean we should allow children, especially in primary grades, to determine what and how they should learn. As educators and parents, we must recognize the important role we need to play in providing age-appropriate experiences for children. We must also intervene to help them understand and discuss what they are experiencing and learning. With this in mind, we must, on occasion, challenge them to push their thinking and reflection into more complicated ideas and issues. We cannot allow them to do all their learning on their own or at their own time. To care, we must intervene and, at times, push them..

Damon adds, "In truth, Piaget was not only a constructivist but also an interactionist. When Piaget wrote that children learn through their own actions, he did not mean that they learn in a vacuum. Essential to the learning process, as Piaget formulated it, was feedback from the child's actions to the real world." (p. 103) "Simply put," he states, "children cannot learn wholly on their own; for intellectual [and I would argue social and moral] growth, they need to be instructed, prodded, challenged, corrected, and assisted by people who are trying to teach them something." (p. 105) Children need love. They also need adults who act as a moral compass and will *show* them right conduct.

Child-centered does not mean child-controlled, and while the needs of the child are paramount, we should apply what we know about how children learn to the classroom. We must instruct and lead. This applies to the intellect as well as the moral or social processes. We must insist on practices that lead to the formation of a good learning and caring community.

In a society that follows certain conventions and requires children to interact with adults, allowing a child to pursue his or her own interests when he or she desires will not work. Children need time to explore ideas and play, but they also need to develop the habits of being respectful, responsible, and caring from our modeling and teaching these traits.

Students need guidance and standards by which to assess their responses. Simply stating what we feel is, by itself, not necessarily enough to sprout good values. Feeling good about a response does not make the response acceptable. Sometimes a statement or a cherished belief is wrong or, at least, misleading. For example, if a child believes that hitting another child in the classroom is appropriate, we must help that child—through dialogue, role playing, or the issuance of a directive—learn that hitting one's peers is wrong and unacceptable. It is not negotiable. Another example may have a child who clearly misinterprets what an author is trying to say in a narrative. It is okay to work with the child to help him correct his interpretation and to better understand what the author was saying.

If we cherish our children, we are obligated to help them acquire good character. By doing so—by helping them learn responsibility, diligence, and self-control, as well as respect for themselves and others—we are preparing them for success in school, in relationships, in careers, in their whole lives. What parent or teacher wouldn't want that for their children? We must activate the "moral circuitry" already present in their systems and teach them and encourage them to become the moral citizens they were born to be. This is done by setting firm limits that will help them work through frustration and obstacles. Damon adds:

> Children must learn to cope with stubborn realities that will not change, as the children's moods and feelings change, and that will not vanish when the children's complaints grow loud enough. Failing to give children firm rules and guidelines is a sure way to breed arrogance and disrespect. It leads to another facet of the inflated sense of self-importance that is fed by our culture's over emphasis on self-esteem. (p. 79)

I believe there are two ways to insure that students become disciplined. One is to model and the other is to practice rules and procedures which, if followed, are beneficial to the smooth functioning of a school and the character development of the students. Following rules and procedures is the primary means to achieving the self-control in students that allows all students a civil, orderly environment in which to pursue their education

To learn more about this, we turn to Dr. Harry and Tripi Wong's work, *The First Days of School* (1991). They write:

1. The most successful classes are those where the teacher has a clear idea of what is expected from the students and the students know what the teacher expects from them.
2. Expectations can be stated as rules.
3. Rules are expectations of appropriate student behavior.
4. After thorough deliberation, decide on your rules and write them down or post them before the first days of school.
5. Communicate clearly to your students what you expect as appropriate behavior.
6. It is easier to maintain good behavior than to change inappropriate behavior that has become established.
7. Rules immediately create a work-oriented atmosphere.
8. Rules create a strong expectation about the things that are important to you. (p. 143)

In other words, rules let students know what is valued in a classroom. The Wongs indicate that there are different kinds of rules. The first type, specific rules, are exacting in nature. They tell you what to do and you do not need any additional explanation. For example, "Pick up the trash around your desk at the end of the class period," does not need any additional explanations. Another specific rule might be "Keep your hands, feet, and objects to yourself." These rules stand by themselves. The same applies to rules like "Place your homework in the basket when you walk into the class." Provide a basket. Label it *Homework* and put it in a convenient location where students entering the classroom can't miss seeing it. Have them put their homework in the basket. After several practices, the students are accustomed to the procedure.

Specific rules usually do not result in much confusion. They are descriptive in nature and give short, quick instructions regarding proper behavior. They describe what is to be done. General rules are different. They prescribe what we ought to do, but don't give specific details about what one should do to live up to the expectations of the rule. For example, the general rule "Treat all persons with respect" provides a fine prescription as to how a child should act, but it does not tell the child what he or she should do to demonstrate of the virtue or the expectation.

For a general rule to have meaning, we must develop procedures that, if followed, will allow the student to develop respectful habits that will lead to compliance with the rule. For example, procedures to follow the general "Be respectful" rule might include "Raise your hand before talking," "Hold the door for the person behind you," and "Say please, thank you, and excuse me." Young children and adolescents can be confused about what it means to treat someone with respect. They may not know how to do this. Have you ever talked with a child who honestly didn't know what he had done wrong, or how his actions were inappropriate? General rules demand procedures to insure clarity, understanding, and consistency for both students and educators to follow them.

In Chapter 3, we will learn more about practicing procedures that will avoid confusion and help the child develop the habits which lead to civility.

R E V I E W

1 We are wired with the potential to be a good person. To activate the "circuitry," children need moral modeling and instruction.

2 Children, left on their own, will not learn to be a moral persons. They need feedback and interaction with caring adults.

3 A child–centered classroom does not mean child–controlled. As adults, we are in charge of insuring that a good caring and learning community exists.

4 Rules facilitate the development of a good climate for children and adults by helping all know what is valued.

RULES & PROCEDURES

PROCEDURES BREATHE LIFE INTO RULES

Procedures are different from rules. While general rules prescribe what we ought to do, and specific rules tell us what to do, procedures describe how things are done. They are the practices or actions needed to follow the rules. Young people always respond better when they're asked to do a specific thing, rather than meet a vague objective. If they know what they're supposed to do, most of them will generally do it. Just this year, my wife Cynthia and I revisited our procedures to help our elementary-age daughter get ready for school. We decided she needed to be up by 6:30, dressed with her hair combed by 6:45, breakfasted by 7:00, and have her teeth brushed and book bag ready to go out the door by 7:10. After several rather interesting mornings, Mary Kathryn caught on, and she now keeps an eye on the clock herself for these intermediate deadlines. The organized procedures have become habits, and she's now always ready for school on time!

Here's a tough question: When do students generally get in trouble—during times of direct instruction or during transitions? Like most educators, you probably answered during transitions. If talking and impolite behavior routinely get out of hand during transitions, the problem is a procedural one, which can be remedied with clear-cut procedures. Students are not thinking "I have to remember to respect others" when they hand up their test papers and leave the classroom. They want to talk to their friends about the test. A teacher who wants to keep order and civility will not be saying, "Respect others, students." She'll be reminding them of the class procedures for handing up papers: "Pass your papers without talking to the front of the room, then file out quietly, please." In that classroom, clearly defined procedures let students know how they're supposed to behave; the teacher's brief reminder keeps everyone on track..

Let's examine that general rule "Respect others." That, or perhaps "Treat everyone with respect," is posted in thousands of schools across the country. Its objective is to yield a body of students who speak courteously to everyone, are on time and prepared for class, and don't intrude in others' space or impose on others' privacy. But most students, especially young ones, don't read all that into the rule. In all grade levels, some students come from homes where family members don't show respect to one another, and the whole concept is new. So how can we lead students into "treating everyone with respect"? We can begin by telling them we expect respectful behavior, and then we explain and demonstrate what respectful behavior looks, sounds, and feels like. They can meet our objective because we have shown them the procedures leading to it. We may choose to have them develop, with our help, their own procedures. In this way, they have input on the procedures and we can have the final say.

What are the procedures students need to practice to acquire the habit of treating people with respect? If we start with being respectful of others in the halls, we establish that students and teachers will stand or move quietly in the halls and not interrupt the learning opportunities of others. To develop the habit of treating others with respect while walking in the halls, we need to establish expectations of the following procedures:

RULE: Treat Everyone with Respect

What are the procedures students need to practice to acquire the habit of treating people with respect? If we start with being respectful of others in the halls, we establish that students and teachers will exhibit quietness in the halls and do not interrupt the learning opportunities of others.

To develop the habit of treating others with respect while walking in the halls, we need to establish expectations of the following:

PROCEDURES

1 Walk on the right side of the hall.

2 Walk quietly in the halls. (In middle and high school, only talking, not yelling during class change. (Because elementary students move throughout the school all day long, they should always move quietly in the halls so others are not disturbed.)

3 Hold the door for those walking behind you to prevent the door from slamming.

4 Keep your hands to yourself

Now you try! The general rule is: **Respect Others.** Write down several procedures that will help students practice respect *in the classroom.*

1. _____

_____

2. _____

_____

3. _____

_____

4. _____

What is another general rule or expectation of appropriate behavior you want students to follow in your classroom? What procedures do they need to learn to develop the habit of following the rule?

GENERAL RULE: _____

Procedures:

1. _____

_____

2. _____

_____

3. _____

_____

4. _____

Notice how in practicing these procedures students are practicing being respectful to others. Through practice, being respectful becomes an acquired habit. The same approach applies to any other positive attribute we wish students and educators to adopt. Practice of virtuous actions helps students internalize the virtue and later apply it in situations they have not practiced.

Look at the rule and procedures you listed above. If students followed these procedures, would they practice actions and develop habits that would allow them to follow the rule? Some educators argue that following rules and procedures isn't all that important. After all, in the total scheme of things, what does the development of small, positive habits do for students? What is the big deal about holding the door open for someone or being respectful toward others in a classroom? James Q. Wilson, in his work, *The Moral Sense* (1993), takes a strong position:

> ...habits, routine ways of acting, each rather unimportant in itself, but taken together, producing action on behalf of quite important sensibilities. For example: the habit of courtesy (which over the long run alerts us to the feelings of others), the habit of punctuality (which disposes us to be dutiful in the exercise of our responsibilities and confirms to others that we have a sense of duty), and the habit of practice (by which we master skills and proclaim to others that we are capable of excellence). (p. 241)

The little habits, practiced daily, help a school function smoothly and mold the character of youth and adults, which makes a great deal of difference in the life of the child. Rules and procedures "set the table" for all future character-developing efforts. Remember our task is to help facilitate the development of good student habits through the use of rules and procedures.

An excellent methodology to help teachers organize the practice of procedures is provided in *Organizing and Managing the Elementary School Classroom* (1981), published by the Research and Development Center for Teacher Education at the University of Texas at Austin. This work recognizes that procedures or actions designed to develop habits in students are important to help them learn to follow rules. Observe how this project uses rules and procedures to help educators focus on what they must consider to facilitate the development of good student habits:

1. **Be polite and helpful.** This may be worded in various ways (e.g., be considerate of others; be courteous). Children must be given examples for this rule to have meaning. They must learn how to be polite and helpful in dealing with adults and each other.

2. **Take care of your school.** This is another very general rule that the teacher must think through before using. The teacher may want to include positive examples, such as picking up trash in the halls or on the school grounds, returning library books on time, and/or such rigidly stated things as not marking on walls, desks, or school books. The teacher must be sure to discuss and follow up with the class whatever detailed behavior is expected from this rule as well as consequences for not following the rule.

Both the Wongs and the Texas Project reveal that just stating the rules isn't enough to develop good character in students. Teachers working individually, with their students, or as a school must determine the procedures needed for students to understand, practice, and develop good habits that make following rules a natural part of their day. State the rules and then make some general comments about the rules. Afterward, the school could determine the procedures needed to develop the habits of following the rules. The Texas project could very well be a model for school-wide rules and procedures.

So far, the discussion has been about rules and procedures being in the domain of educators. Can students help in determining rules and procedures? Absolutely! Students know about the importance of rules as early as preschool. They also may know what they ought to do. The following approaches utilize students' input:

Approach One:

Cynthia Vincent, an elementary teacher in Hickory, N.C., implemented procedures based on her rules regarding being respectful, responsible, and caring toward themselves and others. She started out the school year on the first day by writing the words *Respect, Responsibility*, and *Caring* on her blackboard. She then asked each student what he or she did at home and at school to practice being respectful, responsible, and caring. Each idea was discussed in depth. Afterward, the students created art that illustrated them practicing respect, responsibility, and caring. Ms. Vincent modified her and her students' ideas into a list of procedures they all would follow in the classroom and hall.

On the second day of school, these students began practicing their procedures, diligently continuing through the week. After the first week, the students had developed many of the habits that would allow them to be successful in school. An environment that was good for students as well as the teacher evolved. Vincent continued the focus by having a meeting at the beginning of each school day in order for students to talk about what they could do to be respectful and responsible that day. Time was taken to thank others for what they had done the previous day.

Any "backsliding" was discussed over a class meeting. The students were asked to reflect on what had been occurring in the classroom, and the rules and procedures were reviewed for further reinforcement. Even at elementary age, children are capable of evaluating their behavior and contributing to the class objectives; they fully participated in these class meetings. Procedures that were not being followed consistently were highlighted and extra effort was required.

By implementing procedures for proper behavior in class, Ms. Vincent had a wonderful environment from which to teach and the students had greater opportunities to learn. Finally, as students continued their excellent behavior, they were recognized for their success. Letters were sent home to the parents, and recognition occurred individually or as an entire class. A quiet word, a smile and a nod, or a class celebration is enough.

Approach Two:

Several years ago, Booker T. Washington High School in Pensacola, Florida, used student input to determine some procedures based on the five school rules created to foster a better climate for learning. Shirley Bordelon, a guidance counselor at the school, provides the following description of their efforts:

Teachers, administrators, staff, and 23 Student Government Association leaders and Core Values Team members were randomly divided into groups of 14-16, with at least one or two students in every group. A trained facilitator, the late Pam Shelton, directed the entire process.

First, the groups brainstormed to identify problems and concerns. Each group developed five general rules and wrote them on a flip chart. When each group had completed this, similar rules were combined, and one list of five rules was drafted. The five rules adopted were:

- Show respect for yourself, others and property.
- Demonstrate personal responsibility.
- Obey laws concerning drugs and alcohol.
- Be honest in all you do.
- Contribute to a positive school environment.

The students selected the rule on drugs and alcohol. Just two weeks prior, an outstanding sophomore had been killed in an alcohol/high speed-related car accident. Another Booker T. Washington student was the driver. Some teachers new to the faculty did not feel this rule was appropriate. Much discussion and disagreement took place.

The facilitator later stated that she could feel control of the group waning at this point. Amid teachers confronting one another on whether this was an appropriate rule, two students stood up side-by-side, holding hands and crying as they addressed the group. In essence, they said, "We just lost a friend in an alcohol-related accident. We KNOW what teens do on weekends now, and we know alcohol is a BIG problem. All we ask is that you work with us. We know we can't stop all this behavior, but if you will join us, perhaps, together we can make an impact on some. We don't want to lose another classmate."

Many were crying by this time. They sat down, and teachers and staff began clapping—louder and louder. Needless to say, one of the five rules adopted was related to alcohol.

The custodian also was involved in the development of the rules. It was especially touching when one of the students "high fived" the custodian. It was gratifying to all of the teachers to have been a part of the process and to witness all of the mutual respect being displayed.

The group knew this was only the beginning. One morning the students were given the task of developing three procedures under each of the five general rules. Directions were given over the television broadcasting system by the SGA president. Each first period classroom held a class meeting to establish three specific procedures that described what the students should do to follow the general rules. The teachers facilitated the process, which took about an hour.

Each class then selected two "core values representatives" to bring the procedures to the cafeteria. The next day, during an early release day from school, approximately 160 students were grouped randomly at tables in a huge semicircle. Two teachers facilitated the process, assisted by six students who were Escambia County Core Value Team members, a student group that traveled throughout the schools and community stressing the importance of having good core values. Basically, they followed the same process that the faculty and students had done earlier when developing the five general rules.

The student body included advanced placement to special education students, with equal representation of gender, race, and socioeconomic levels. What these students did was incredible! They shared ideas, defended their choices, questioned others and learned how to come to consensus. They became so enthusiastically involved that the processes were not complete when school was dismissed at 10:30 on an early release day. The principal allowed the same group of students to meet again on Friday morning for the first time block (90 minutes) to complete their work.

Shirley Bordelon wrote: "Students claim ownership in rules and practices when they are the authors. With a little guidance, I believe they did a much better job than a group of us adults could have done. Their rules are from the heart—that was obvious during the process.

"It just reinforced what I already believe. Our youth are the greatest. Give them Respect, give them a chance to assume Responsibility, treat them with Equality, react to them with

Honesty and Integrity, and they will respond with tremendous Patriotism. B.T. Washington High School is a school reaching for realms beyond what could have been imagined three years ago. We are *indeed a school on the move in the right direction with our students.*"

This school's approach to character development could serve as a guide for other middle and high school staff wanting to create the same processes. It appears that the students knew that, in developing these rules, they would not be limiting their control; rather, they would be assisting in creating the type of school environment they desired.

The process would be the same with elementary students as described in Approach One. Teachers, administrators, and parents usually start the process, followed by the input of the students to establish the practices. This is the beginning of children creating their own destinies.

R E V I E W

1 Rules are expectations of appropriate student behavior. Procedures are the practices needed to develop the habits of good behavior or virtues.

2 Children need to be disciplined. By this we mean they need to follow rules by using agreed-upon procedures. Discipline helps them develop good habits.

3 There are general and specific rules. General rules prescribe how we ought to act (e.g., "Respect others."). Specific rules tell us exactly what we should do (e.g., "Put your homework in the basket as you walk in the classroom door.").

4 To avoid confusion with rules, especially general rules, we must link them to procedures that help to develop the habits needed to follow the rules.

5 Students can contribute to this endeavor, but they are not participants in a total democracy. The educational establishment must insure an environment where learning can occur. However, this process should not dismiss student contributions, nor their abilities to focus on key rules and procedures.

6 It helps to post the procedures stating how students are expected to behave, not just the general rules. Both are needed to remind students of good behavior.

RULES & PROCEDURES

4

THE USE OF CONSEQUENCES IN BUILDING CHARACTER

My involvement with school districts around the country reveals that the majority of school personnel desire to help children develop good habits. They want to address rules and procedures that offer good practices and hold students accountable. This short discourse will clarify the importance of rules and procedures, offering guidelines on how to use the consequences of not following rules and procedures to encourage good habits in their students.

This chapter will not satisfy everyone. Some may argue that if we let kids find their own way with minimal adult supervision, they will grow into solid students and citizens. There are times when a child may need less adult supervision. Adults must provide more autonomy for the child as he matures. However, this does not divorce adults from the life of the child. James Q. Wilson, in *The Moral Sense* (1993), notes:

> Testing limits is a way of asserting selfhood. Maintaining limits is a way of asserting community. If the limits are asserted weakly, uncertainly, or apologetically, their effects must surely be weaker than if they are asserted boldly, confidently and persuasively. (p. 9)

The expectations of appropriate behavior should be expected and exemplified by the child even when he or she is away from immediate supervision. An acquaintance and her husband told me that, when her teenagers leave the house, she inquires where her teens are going, who they will be with, and when they will be home. The teens also leave with one rule: "Have responsible fun—no drinking, drugs, or sex!" The teens laugh about this, but their parents' insistence that habits of respect and responsibility to others and themselves is reinforced by this reminder. Children need the constant involvement of parents and other adults to act as moral compasses to keep them acting with good judgment, even when pressured by peers or situations.

There are various strategies we can use to enhance this compass. We can talk with our children or students. Sharing ideas about how we think a good person would act and time-tested parables and stories such as Aesop's fables, or from *Reader's Digest* or the *Chicken Soup for the Soul* books is important in the lives of children. We can insist on the development of good habits in our children at home, in the community and school, and we can enforce consequences for behaviors we deem inappropriate. Good habits include courtesy to others, picking up your own dirty clothes, and completing homework before playing on the computer. Consequences might be loss of allowance for failing to complete obligations, or being grounded for a weekend for telling a lie. Some may feel that consequences or punishment of children are unnecessary, that we should just model what we feel is important and sit down and talk with them when some issue comes up.

Modeling right conduct and practicing good habits are the most important ways to teach civil behavior to children. Other times, teaching traits like good manners must be practiced over and over. How many times have you reminded your children to say please? Other politenesses must be suggested as occasions arise ("When someone gives you a gift, even if you don't like it, you are obligated to show appreciation for the gesture" or "It would be good of you to open the door for that woman carrying the baby"). Discussions with young people over enacting rules and procedures are important, yet there are also times when the consequences of one's inappropriate actions must be confronted. Learning that there are consequences for certain behaviors, and that these consequences may be called punishment, has a vital place in building character in our youth.

Let's briefly examine the definitions of punishment and consequences. Synonyms of punishment are discipline and correction. According to *The New World Dictionary of the American Language, Second College Edition* (1986):

> ...discipline suggests punishment that is intended to control or to establish habits of self-control [to discipline a naughty child]; correct suggests punishment for the purpose of overcoming faults [to correct unruly pupils].

This is exactly what punishment should mean for schools: to help students establish self-control, which enables them to overcome faults that may result in a disruption of the learning environment for all students.

Consequence is defined as "1. a result of an action, process, etc., outcome, effect. 2. a logical result or conclusion: inference." Synonyms of consequence are effect or value. For example, if one assumes the consequences of one's actions, one will accept the "results of one's actions." Awareness of consequences implies that, if one chooses to misbehave, one will accept the logical result (punishment) for one's actions. In this case, consequences are the punishment, and punishment reflects the consequences.

Consider this consequence: "Students who continue to skip middle or high school classes will not be allowed to easily make up their work." We might argue that it's illogical because, as one concerned parent says, "If they can't quickly make up their work they will fail the course." A teacher might contend: "Skipping school results in students being behind in their work. We should provide ample opportunity for them to make up their work." I see the point, but I must answer, "Rubbish!" They have chosen to skip school. Enabling them to make up their work easily may reinforce the behavior. It's the student's responsibility to get the assignments and make up the work—and on the student's time! It's not the teacher's job to bend over backwards to help a student who chose to skip class. If the behavior continues, additional privileges of the student should be revoked.

My argument is that attending school is a privilege. The privilege assumes that one does one's duty by attending school. If making up school work is made easy for the students who choose to skip school, then what is the consequence for skipping school? This places the consequence and burden of the misbehavior on the teacher, not the student. What is the child learning? Will this learned behavior carry into the world of work?

Clearly, there are exceptions—many students miss school for legitimate reasons—but exceptions must not become the rule. The development of habits of attendance and the responsibility of completing assignments and doing good work in schools are character traits that will pay off over a student's lifetime. The school's role is to expect and reinforce accountability and civility. Honor the rules or face the consequences.

Let's say a student curses at a teacher. This is a serious offense, which calls for immediate consequences. We can talk to the student privately and discover what caused him to make such an outburst, though it may be quite clear from the context. We can suggest ways to avoid this behavior in the future ("I understand you're angry I won't extend your due date, but you may not speak to me in that manner. You could have said...."). But there must be some consequences for the action, or we are telling him, along with 30 other eagerly attentive students, that cursing at a teacher is acceptable behavior, which it is not. The consequence should be immediately called for, preferably in front of the same people who witnessed the improper behavior ("You will apologize to me and to the rest of the class for your language now, and you will see me after class to receive an extra assignment."). There is a time for counseling/talking, and there is a time for consequences/punishment.

Some educators maintain that a child who continually challenges school rules is begging for help. If this is so, school staff should do all possible to help by providing counseling and support. In providing support to the student, school staff must also insist that student follow the rules or face the consequences. Expectations of appropriate behavior during the class period should not be compromised because we cannot meet the emotional needs of a student with underlying personal problems.

Educators frequently ask me if I really believe in enforcing consequences that result in punishment. My answer is emphatically yes, if a student chooses to break the rules or refuses to follow the procedures established in school. The key word here is *chooses*. The majority of students know what they are doing and choose to do it, even those students we consider to be "emotionally handicapped." (An atypical situation might be if a severely handicapped child, whose abilities to make decisions may be compromised, contributes to various interruptions.) My experiences with grades K-12 have exposed me to educators who have created caring learning environments with almost any kind of child in their class—no matter what the child's classification.

As educators, we are obligated to meet the educational needs of all students. They expect and respond the most positively if the administration and faculty are consistent, caring, and fair in providing a favorable learning environment. What's important is insuring a safe, consistent environment for children to learn both the academics and social traits needed for good citizenship.

Children naturally respond well in classes where teachers have high expectations, caring environments, and solid instructional strategies that include the practice of rules and procedures designed to help students achieve academic and social goals. These teachers let all students know what school and class rules and procedures are. Their students know they're responsible for their work and their behavior. Most students, even those with behavioral problems, want to do well and be liked by others.

Anne Jenkins is a prime example of a teacher with high expectations. She stresses parental involvement and discipline with her 20 kindergarten students at Diggs Elementary School in Winston-Salem, N.C. According to Kristin Scheve, writing for the *Winston-Salem Journal* (June 7, 1997), parents praised Ms. Jenkins for her emphasis on discipline and expressed pride that their children were already reading at the end of the school year.

Skilled educators like Ms. Jenkins encourage the practice of regular procedures, knowing firsthand that the procedures may not go smoothly with all students. These teachers are also willing to use consequences for students who choose to disrupt the learning environment for others. The consequences can start with a gentle pat on the back or a stare to help focus the child on the appropriate behavior. Occasionally it may require a discussion in the back of the class or even in the hall. Sometimes a call home results in cessation of a child's negative behaviors. What is important is that the child knows the teachers will follow through with consequences. Even students with behavioral problems are expected to achieve steady improvement from the beginning of school to the end of the year. In this safe environment, most students will make progress, even if their home lives are deteriorating. The classroom becomes a haven of stability. Using punishment/consequence is the last alternative, but it can and should be used. Whether it's one teacher at a time or school teams who are committed to providing a structured caring environment for their students, both have consistent school-wide procedures they follow to engender warm, learning environments.

School teams at Arndt Middle School in Hickory, N.C., are responsible for office referrals dropping from nearly ten per day to fewer than one per day over a five-year period. The teams work hard to develop a consistent school-wide structure that insures a caring environment for the students. Students who choose to misbehave will encounter some of the consequences listed above. If the students continue to misbehave, they must "face the team." Misbehaving students must sit down with the team members during team planning. The principal or guidance counselor may attend the conference, along with the elective teacher who is also committed to the process. The elective teacher usually gets someone to cover his class.

The meeting to face the team consists of serious discussions with the student. It is not intended to be a pleasant conference, its clinical function being to determine what action must be taken to stop the present behavior. The teachers talk with the student, but are polite, unemotional, and very firm about their expectations. They remind the student of the consequences that will occur if disruptive behavior continues. The school's data indicate that most students (over 80 percent) who face the team never need to come back to a session.

Students who still choose not to follow procedures, even after efforts of educators, must face consequences if a school is to maintain an orderly climate, and if students are to learn responsibility. Educators must not shy away from punishment when students show a disregard for civility, such as striking another student, disrupting other students' learning, or speaking rudely to a teacher.

Edward Wynne and Kevin Ryan, in their book *Reclaiming Our Schools: A Handbook on Teaching Character, Academics, and Discipline*, 2nd Edition (1997), stress the important role of consequences for students who choose to misbehave. They emphasize that effective punishments or consequences must have certain characteristics:

1. They must be clearly disliked by students—they must deter.

2. They must not absorb large amounts of school resources (e.g., schools cannot afford to assign a full-time paid adult monitor for each disobedient pupil).

3. They must be capable of being applied in "doses" of increasing severity.

4. They must not be perceived as cruel.

5. In public schools, they often must be applicable without strong cooperation from the parent of the pupil involved.

6. They must be able to be applied quickly—the next day, or even within one minute of the infraction, instead of the next week. (p. 98)

The authors provide a long list of effective punishments or consequences. Some of their ideas are:

1. Subjecting pupils to before- or after-school detention within 24 hours of their violation (or, as one school found, Saturday detentions for more serious offenses, since they interrupted student's Saturday games and jobs).

2. Providing an in-school suspension in a designated room, supervised by a stern monitor, with chitchat prohibited and students assigned to do their missed class work.

3. Sharply and suddenly (and sometimes publicly) criticizing individual pupils for particular immediate acts of misconduct, such as treating another student harshly.

4. Having erring pupils write notes to their parents explaining their misconduct, and having them promptly return the notes, signed by their parents.

5. Automatically calling the police whenever any student's conduct violates the criminal law. (p. 100)

You may disagree with Wynne and Ryan's selection of consequences. But would it not be unconscionable to allow students to act inappropriately time after time, when practicing character traits such as courtesy, respect, and responsibility will help them in their lives? If modeling, practicing, teacher dialoguing, and peer pressure don't work, then consequences must be applied. The authors offer many other excellent examples of consequences for refusing to follow rules and procedures. They also caution us to be fair in meting out consequences, which in this instance means following school or school board policies and applying the same consequences to all students.

This doesn't mean that we shouldn't consider the circumstances resulting in a child's misconduct. A child who is going through a rough time may need extra attention and acknowledgment of his or her difficulties. Staff should be made aware of these situations, and extra help afforded in suggesting more appropriate behavior. Peer helpers can be enlisted to spend additional time with the child. Our main thrust is assisting all students and providing them with nurturing environments from which to learn. Still, consequences for inappropriate behavior must be considered and applied.

If cursing at a teacher is an offense that is supposed to result in a three- to five-day suspension, then suspend the child. You may counsel the child before the suspension and continue this after the suspension, but the suspension must occur. This is fair and motivates the child to learn appropriate ways to channel his or her anger before serious problems arise. In many cases, the child gets so much more pressure and additional discipline at home that the misbehavior problem is cured, but we can't count on that.

We send a terrible message to students if consistent rules and procedures aren't being followed, particularly at the high school and middle school levels. Students are constantly looking for order and fairness in their lives and they'll spot inequities as if they were blinking neon roadway signs. The following example addresses the issue of consistency:

> Football is very important for the students and the community at Main High School. A senior player on the football team, Will, broke a school rule involving skipping class, which earned him a one-day suspension. Unfortunately, he broke this rule on a Friday, and since he was suspended that day (actually any suspension during a week results in a suspension for the remainder of that week's after-school activities), he could not participate in that night's football game. This was especially difficult since it was homecoming, but he knew what would happen if he broke the rule.
>
> Several weeks later during the league championship games, Tom, the quarterback, was caught skipping class. The principal decided to hold off the suspension until Monday and allow Tom to quarterback for the team on Friday. Since they did not play the following week, the team would not be hurt.

Word seeped out to the students, who became angry about the unfair treatment. They wanted to win the football game, but fair was fair. To their way of thinking, if Will had been suspended for the same offense, Tom should also be suspended. The students at Main High School "learned" from the principal's handling of this incident that who you are determines how you will be treated. If we truly want a "level playing field" for all students, then we have to make every effort as consistent as possible.

The students took their case to the community and eventually the school board. They spoke of fairness and modeling of consistency. By not being consistent, the principal lost the respect of the students and much of the faculty. He resigned at the end of the year. If cutting class results in a one-day suspension, then enforce the consequence.

This issue of consistency is not just an administrative problem. It extends to teachers throughout the school. Elementary teachers face special problems with students who are in the halls all day, going to lunch, foreign language classes, P.E., music, art, special education, etc. Students need to know that any teacher, teacher assistant, custodian, librarian, office staff member, or administrator may admonish students for not following rules, and may single a child out for consequences. Consistent modeling and reinforcement of procedures by all adults enable students to move back and forth in orderly ways. Young students who are unable to follow the procedures in the beginning, may need additional opportunities to develop the habits that will enable them to be successful. However, if they continue to disrupt the classroom environment, appropriate punishment should occur.

Many primary teachers have found that the consequence of not allowing children time to play at recess, using this time instead as a time-out to develop better habits of behavior, is a powerful encouragement to better behavior. This punishment is not cruel, but it does make a powerful point. The child knows if he chooses to misbehave, he'll miss his fun.

Middle schools similarly have special areas of concern, because of the team framework in which they work. Teams can consist of two to five teachers who must try to develop consistent rules and procedures that are used and followed by all team students and teachers. Clearly, they must all follow school rules, but they may have specific team procedures. This helps insure consistency throughout the school day.

From an administrative point of view, if one teacher in the middle school team has far more office referrals than other team members, most likely this teacher needs some assistance in becoming more congruent in following the established rules and procedures and, if needed, applying consequences. If it were a student body problem, the number of office referrals would be the same for all team members.

We must also assess the climate of the class to determine if it is an inviting one for students and adults. Is there genuine love between the teacher and the students? It's impossible to like every child we teach, but we're required to love every child we teach. Notice the difference. If we simply like children, we can excuse poor behavior, just as we excuse poor behavior of some friends. But if we love students, we must help them do the right thing by modeling, talking, sharing and, if necessary, punishing.

Adding to Wynne and Ryan's assessments on effective consequences is the use of *time-out*. Generally speaking, time-out involves the teacher or the student through her own initiative, removing a student from a trying situation to assess and determine the right course of action. During time-out a child may quietly sit and reflect on the previous events. The child can contemplate and, if necessary, write out what is needed to rejoin the group in a more controlled manner. Depending on the age and maturity of the child, the child may rejoin the group without permission of the teacher or may need to talk with the teacher and describe her plan of action before rejoining the group. The focus on time-out should be on the student determining, perhaps with the help of a teacher, the appropriate steps to take to insure success in the group once again.

Diane Chelsom Gossen incorporates restitution, having a student "make right" a particular wrong, as another method of possible punishments that allows the student to compensate for hurt or damage to another person. It's a way to put the poor choice and misbehavior in the past. One of the best examples on restitution can be viewed in episode 101 of "The Andy Griffith Show," a television series available on video. It's titled "Opie the Birdman." Richard Kelly, writing in *The Andy Griffith Show* (1981) describes Opie's careless actions and punishment:

> ...Opie, after being warned by his father to be careful how he used his new slingshot, carelessly killed a mother bird, leaving her babies helpless. Andy goes to Opie's room, and outside the window can be heard the cries of the little birds. Andy says, "I'm not going to give you a

whipping." He turns and opens the window and says, "Do you hear that? That's them young birds chirping for their mama that's never coming back. And you just listen to that for awhile."

Opie had to learn how to rear the three young birds, which became his restitution for accidentally killing their mother. As a result, Opie inherited two important character by-products: respect for life and a responsibility for his actions.

In *Restitution: Restructuring School Discipline* (1992), Gossen argues that teachers should encourage children to seek solutions to problems that would normally demand teacher intervention or consequences. For example, a child wrongs another child. The teacher does not immediately punish the child. Instead, the child who committed the offense works to make things right with the offended child, as Opie made things right with the baby birds and his father. A child who is capable of restituting another child must have several characteristics:

1. S/he must have a sense of right and wrong.
2. S/he must acknowledge that s/he did wrong to another.
3. S/he must be capable of developing an action which will make the wrong right and this action must be agreed upon by the offended and the teacher.

There is always the exception and, in this case, it involves students who are unable or unwilling to admit infractions, or those who feel everything that happens to them is someone else's fault. In these cases, teacher-enforced consequences are still necessary, especially since some actions need immediate intervention. Students who have never been taught what it means to be respectful of others or be responsible for their own actions are at a disadvantage. This is why educators must take the time to go over rules and procedures with students at the beginning of each year. They should solicit and incorporate student input because it will strengthen student buy-in to the importance of rules and procedures to create a civil and orderly climate and, ideally, it will enhance student adherence to the rules and procedures.

Extensive practice may be necessary for younger students—keep in mind how often you have to remind your own young children to say thank you, pick up their toys, close the door gently. Older students who have been in a character-developing environment emphasizing the practice of good rules and procedures should be praised for their success and encouraged to continue their habits. Newcomers should receive an orientation session on the school's rules and procedures facilitated by the principal, assistant principal, counselor, teacher, or peers. Perhaps the best method is to have a combination of the above educators working to make students and their parents aware of the rules, procedures and if necessary, the consequences within the school environment.

The effort to achieve civility in a school by following rules and procedures will only be as effective as the effort to enforce consequences of breaking the rules.

REVIEW

1 Punishment and consequences are not dirty words. There are times when students must be punished for their actions. Rules aren't rules if there is no consequence for flouting them.

2 Punishment must not be cruel and demeaning. This doesn't mean it should be ineffective. It just means that we should treat the misbehaver with respect because we at all times should be modeling the behavior we want students to learn. And students are always watching how we treat them.

3 The punishment must be administered in a timely manner. It makes little sense to issue punishment for a days-old incident.

4 The climate of the classroom can aid or stunt the development of good procedures and habits.

5 Some students may have the ability to "restitute" others for their offenses. If you can agree upon the restitution, this is a good lesson for students to learn.

6 What we have learned about rules and procedures and motivational theory thus far will help us to develop our own practices to cultivate character awareness in students.

RULES & PROCEDURES

5

INITIATING RULES AND PROCEDURES IN YOUR SCHOOL

Perhaps now you're ready to begin a character development program in your school. Where to begin? Start by asking, "What character traits or positive habits should students have when they leave our school?" Your school may have already adopted a list of character traits for good citizenship from your district office. If not, you can initiate the process by setting up meetings and inviting peers and community members to discuss various character traits that to consider. A good first step is to look over the sequence of activities that others have used sucessfully.

One way to approach the procedures for enlisting community support and establishing a character education program is outlined in *Character Education Workbook For School Boards, Administrators & Community Leaders*, available from Character Development Group.

The Character Counts Coalition is a national association that has the support of 80 leading character-building organizations such as the YMCA, 4-H, Boy and Girl Scouts, and the American Federation of Teachers. Many school programs have adopted their key traits—trustworthiness, respect, responsibility, caring, fairness and citizenship, which they call the Six Pillars of Character—as the ones most valuable to cultivate in our children. These universally appealing traits might meet your needs, and might be the ones your faculty and community can most easily reach consensus on. Other schools choose honesty instead of trustworthiness, or service instead of citizenship. Others value self-control as a key trait. You will be on solid ground by making the six pillars your foundation, even if the school or district adds additional traits. The point is to choose the traits that mean the most to *your* school and community.

Once consensus has been reached on the core character traits, the next step is to establish rules and procedures that will yield the desired trait. As a staff member, you and your committee, which may include administrators, parents and students would begin with one of the selected character traits, say responsibility, and ask a question such as, "What specific practices are needed to help students learn to act responsibly towards themselves and others?" Do this with each of the selected traits, and soon you and your committee will have a list of practices under each trait. From these desirable practices come the rules and procedures for your school.

Let's follow the example all the way through: You have selected responsibility as a core trait. What practices develop responsible behavior? Walking quietly in the halls, keeping the lunchroom clean, speaking respectfully to both teachers and peers, keeping hands and feet to oneself, not disturbing study hall...you can make quite a list. For your school, you might choose respect as a core trait. The written rule might be "Treat others with respect," and the written procedures might include "Speak respectfully to all others in the school," "Do not disturb the study of other students," and "Pick up after yourself in the lunchroom."

By putting this theory into practice, the rules become the written expectations of good behavior; both teachers and students know what acceptable behavior in school is. Following the rules through practicing the procedures will lead to a school climate that is calmer, safer, more civil, and more beneficial to academic progress. Both teachers and students will enjoy and benefit permanently from the change.

Developing rules and procedures will require building positive, cohesive relationships within the group. Joe Hester, in his book *Bridges: Building Relationships and Resolving Conflicts* (1995), cites the work of Adler and Rodman (1982) as an important tool in helping us understand the process of conflict resolution. Below are keys for keeping the group—that is, the school or district—going forward on the process of developing rules and procedures. I have added additional comments in brackets.

1 **Shared goals.** People draw closer when they share a similar purpose or when their goals can be mutually satisfied. [The group, led by a facilitator, must acknowledge the goals and the potential for meeting them.]

2 **Progress toward these goals.** While a group is making progress, members feel highly cohesive. [Make sure that the progress of the group is visible. Write down what is said. If a particular idea demands discussion, then discuss it, but all efforts must be focused on working toward a solution, not a debate.]

3 **Shared norms and values.** While successful groups will tolerate, and even thrive on, some differences in member attitudes and behaviors, wide variations in the group's definition of what actions or beliefs are proper will reduce cohesiveness. [The group must stay focused on what is being done and agree to work together. As mentioned above, difficult points can be discussed, but discussion shouldn't stop progress. Move on, and come back to sticky points later. Above all, seek consensus.]

4 **Lack of perceived threat between members.** A cohesive group is usually one in which members see no threat to their status, dignity, and material or emotional well-being. [Members are not there to blame others for previous failures. Sessions are not for pointing fingers, but for problem-solving.]

5 **Interdependence of members.** Groups become cohesive when their needs can be satisfied with the help of the other members. [By working together, each

individual can achieve his or her goals. Individual growth occurs through connecting with other members of the group.]

In recent years, I have been fortunate to work with educators around the country as they struggle to develop consistent rules and procedures to foster a civil climate in their schools. I use the word "struggle" because if we have learned anything it is this: Teachers must also struggle to define what rules and procedures they will consistently teach and model for the students. Just because we are a school doesn't mean we have developed consistent expectations of appropriate student and teacher behavior. We need to go through some steps to insure consistency and success for ourselves and out students. The forms that follow this chapter will help you do this. If you are working just for your own class, Forms 1 and 5 will be adequate. If you are working—and I hope you are—at gaining continuity across the entire school, you will need to use all the forms. You will need to work in groups of four to six educators to have the best success.

The following forms are useful if the faculty is working to determine the general rules and procedures of the school. Each of the eight forms has a specific purpose.

Form 1 reflects the individual work page for general rules. Remember, specific rules generally are clear and do not cause misunderstandings. The students or teachers may choose not to follow them, but they are clear! The general rules demand procedures. Form 1 requires individual attention. Each person must reflect and determine the three to five general rules that will have the most positive impact on the school. Most individuals will state that being respectful and responsible are two general rules worth following. Filling out this form should only take three to five minutes.

Form 2 requires consensus in the group of four to six educators. Choose one person as the group scribe. Each person must share what general rules he or she thinks will most benefit the school. List everyone's general rules. If someone mentions a previously stated rule, acknowledge that it has been stated. For example, one could state being respectful to others several ways. The scribe should place a check mark beside each repeated general rule. This helps the group know what rules have the greatest initial support.

Form 3 is used to reduce the group's general rules down to three to five. Sometimes a small group of six will produce ten or more general rules. These must be chiseled down. Many times this is quite easy. For example you may have a rule concerning being respectful and another about being polite. You may put politeness under respect and develop procedures for the general rule of being respectful by including what politeness looks like. Remember all you are establishing on Form 3 are the expectations. Procedures come later.

Form 4 will include a list of three to five general rules from each small group. Put checks besides the duplicate rules. This will help you see what rules have garnered the greatest consensus. If you are working within a small faculty, you may be able to list your general rules on an overhead and then cut and add until you get your three to five. If you have a larger faculty you may need another procedure. I would recommend that you have some faculty representatives gather over the next several days and hammer out the general rules of the school. These can then be shared through school mail. During the next faculty meeting, you can seek consensus. Remember, seeking consensus does not mean that everyone agrees. It just means that we will follow the will of the majority unless it violates ethical norms. When this is completed, list your final general rules on Form 4. From this you will begin working on your procedures.

Form 5 represents the individual work page on procedures. Treat this just like Form 1 except you will determine the procedures under each of the agreed-upon general rules. For example, if you have four general rules, you must individually determine the procedures that you think would help the school improve its civility.

Form 6 requires reaching consensus in each small group on the procedures under each general rule. This will take some time since there are three to five general rules. Follow the same practice as you did on Form 2. Seek input from everyone. List the procedures at first; you can combine and omit practices later. This form is for getting the variety of procedures down on paper.

Form 7 will demand some give and take on the part of the small-group participants. You want three to five practices under each general rule. Most likely you have many more proposed practices. You must seek consensus. This is achieved by asking, What practices would make the greatest difference in the civility of your school? This question should help you as you develop three to five procedures under each general rule. Take your time on this, for this is crucial. Remember, the procedures must be understandable by educators, students, and parents.

Form 8 will list the procedures under each general rule from the small groups. Duplicate procedures should receive a check mark to denote general consensus. At this point you have two choices. If you are a small faculty, you may be able to reach consensus and write this on Form 9. If you are a larger faculty, I recommend referring this to committee and requesting that the committee work towards consensus, communicate with the faculty via mail, and then prepare for a discussion during the next faculty meeting.

Form 9 is the final installment of the process. This is what gives your final general rules and procedures that everyone in the school will model, practice and teach to everyone else. This helps insure continuity of your efforts towards increased civility in school. This can be shared with the students and parents. You may request comments from each group. However, your hard work should stand and should guide the faculty and students for years to come.

One important note: Please take time to educate and train new faculty on the importance of this document. If you have a 10% retirement or resignation from a faculty per year, in five years you will statistically turned over 50% of your faculty. All new faculty must be brought up to speed on the importance of consistent rules and procedures to promote school civility.

Will this process work? Archer Elementary is located in Greensboro, North Carolina. In the school year 1997-98, it had approximately 500 physical restraints of students. Test scores were among the lowest in the district. In the recent past, it averaged a huge turnover in staff per year. There was minimal parental support in and for the school.

Under the leadership of Darcy Kemp, the school administrators decided to focus on establishing a climate where civility character would grow. To do this they decided to focus on rules and procedures. Have they been successful? At the end of 1999, they assessed their efforts. The data indicated something had happened:

- Physical restraints went from approximately 500 during 1997-98 to only two during the 1998-99 school year.

- Composite data indicated a growth from 55.8% of the students rated at level 3 or 4 (3 means consistent mastery and 4 means superior mastery of the curriculum in reading and mathematics, based on standardized data from state-designed tests in North Carolina to assess preparedness for the next year's curriculum) in the school year 1997-98 to 60.7% rated at level 3 or 4 in the 1998-99 school year.

- All but two teachers requested to come back for the 1999-2000 school year. (One accepted a career promotion move, and the part-time physical education teacher moved to full-time physical education position.) For the first time in several years, there were requests to transfer *to* the school.

- There was a large increase in PTA involvement.

- Civility dominates the entire school.

During the 1999-2000 school year, Ms. Kemp and the staff plan to have even a greater number of students working at level 3 and 4. They also plan to continue and improve their climate of civility. What this school learned is that if teachers have more time to teach, students have more time to learn. Rules and procedures are the first step in school civility and also academic growth.

The process of building rules and procedures at your school will take several months to complete. Parents will appreciate efforts to implement the project for their children. Include the parents by alerting them that the process is going on and seeking additional input from them before issuing the final product. Certain members of the community may like to participate in the endeavor as well.

The real test, though, begins when students start practicing these character-developing procedures and teachers model and seek consistency across all grade levels. We must recognize students who are developing the good practices and encourage those who are struggling. Above all, we must be consistent.

Formulating rules and procedures requires that participants use common sense, but that doesn't mean it's easy. Though parents are perfectly clear on the important role procedures have in the development of good children, many times educators forget. Our focus has been on the rules. Far too many schools have assumed that students either knew the procedures or would quickly learn them. Experience tells us that many children may know the rules, but still struggle to practice the correct procedures. There are times when a child honestly doesn't know what he did wrong. Procedures and their practices help minimize these occurrences. Procedures are the foundation of any character development program because they let students know what behavior is expected of them. Procedures make following rules understandable and possible. Establishing rules and procedures, and consistently enforcing them is the first and most important step toward school civility.

R E V I E W

1   Rules are expectations of student behavior. They should be developed with the understanding that, upon following rules by practicing procedures, students are developing the good character traits we want them to learn.

2   Procedures help students develop the practices needed to form the habits of good character. They are developed by asking, "What procedures must students practice in order to develop the habits of good character?"

3   The more consistent a classroom, school, and school district are in developing and practicing procedures, the greater the chances for students to develop good character.

4   Consequences for not following rules must be established and enforced. Seek consensus on what will occur when a child chooses to disobey a rule or refuses to follow established procedures. Work to insure the consequences are fair and enforceable.

5   Good rules and procedures will make the lives of educators and students much better. If you hesitate in considering establishing new rules and procedures, ask yourself, "Do I want to continue my career working in the present environment under the same circumstances?" If you want to improve the climate of your school you must begin somewhere. Rules and procedures, practiced to develop good habits in children, are the first step toward civility.

FORMS

CHAPTER

TOOLS FOR PLANNING AND IMPLEMENTING RULES AND PROCEDURES

FORM 1 — GENERAL RULES

Individual Work Page for General Rules

Brainstorm a list of general rules. At this point just get your ideas down. You will combine and omit some in the next step.

Combining the General Rules

Develop three to five general rules you wish to share with your group.

1. _____

_____

_____

2. _____

_____

_____

3. _____

_____

_____

4. _____

_____

_____

5. _____

_____

_____

FORM 2 — GENERAL RULES

Small Group's List of General Rules

Share your general rules with the small group of four to six educators. Each person's general rule will be written down below. Do not duplicate the general rules. Just put a check mark beside duplicate ones. You may need additional space.

List your general rules from the small group.

1.

_____

_____

_____

2.

_____

_____

_____

3.

_____

_____

_____

4.

_____

_____

_____

5.

_____

_____

_____

FORM 3 — GENERAL RULES

Small Group's Consensus on General Rules

Examine the small group's general rules from Form 2. Combine and delete until you can reach consensus on three to five general rules. These will be shared with the total group.

Group Consensus

List your three to five general rules that the small group concurs on.

1. _____

_____

_____

2. _____

_____

_____

3. _____

_____

_____

4. _____

_____

_____

5. _____

_____

_____

FORM 4 — GENERAL RULES

Total Group's Consensus on General Rules

Examine the small group's general rules. Combine and delete until your entire large group can reach consensus on three to five general rules.

Group Consensus

List your three to five general rules that the total group concurs on.

1. _____

_____

_____

2. _____

_____

_____

3. _____

_____

_____

4. _____

_____

_____

5. _____

_____

FORM 5 — PROCEDURES

Individual Work Page on Procedures

Taking the total group's three to five general rules, write two to four procedures or practices under each rule. This will be shared with the small group.

GENERAL RULE 1

_____

Procedures

1.

_____

_____

2.

_____

_____

3.

_____

_____

4.

_____

_____

5.

_____

GENERAL RULE **2** (FORM 5: Individual Work Page on Procedures)

_____

Procedures

1. _____

_____

_____

2. _____

_____

_____

3. _____

_____

_____

4. _____

_____

_____

5. _____

_____

_____

GENERAL RULE 3 (FORM 5 Individual Work Page on Procedures)

___

Procedures

1. _____

___

___

2. _____

___

___

3. _____

___

___

4. _____

___

___

5. _____

___

___

GENERAL RULE 4 (FORM 5 Individual Work Page on Procedures)

_____

Procedures

1. _____

_____

_____

2. _____

_____

_____

3. _____

_____

_____

4. _____

_____

_____

5. _____

_____

_____

Procedures

1. _____

_____

_____

2. _____

_____

_____

3. _____

_____

_____

4. _____

_____

_____

5. _____

_____

_____

FORM 6—PROCEDURES

Small Group's Work Page on Procedures

List the total group's three to five general rules below. In small groups again, write procedures under each rule with each member sharing his or her ideas. Don't duplicate the procedures. If it has been said, just put a check beside it to denote agreement.

GENERAL RULE 1 (FORM 6: Small Group's Work Page on Procedures)

_____

Procedures

1. _____

_____

_____

2. _____

_____

_____

3. _____

_____

_____

4. _____

_____

_____

5. _____

Procedures

1.

2.

3.

4.

5.

GENERAL RULE **3** (FORM 6: Small Group's Work Page on Procedures)

Procedures

1.

2.

3.

4.

5.

GENERAL RULE 4 (FORM 6: Small Group's Work Page on Procedures)

Procedures

1.
_____

_____

_____

2.
_____

_____

_____

3.
_____

_____

_____

4.
_____

_____

_____

5.
_____

_____

_____

_____

Procedures

1. _____

_____

_____

2. _____

_____

_____

3. _____

_____

_____

4. _____

_____

_____

5. _____

_____

_____

FORM 7— PROCEDURES

Small Group's Consensus on Rules and Procedures

Take the entire list of rules agreed to on Form 4, and develop two to four procedures or practices under each rule. This will be the final work of of the small group.

GENERAL RULE 1 (FORM 7: Small Group's Consensus on Rules and Procedures)

Procedures

1.

2.

3.

4.

5.

Procedures

1.

2.

3.

4.

5.

Procedures

1. _____

_____

_____

2. _____

_____

_____

3. _____

_____

_____

4. _____

_____

_____

5. _____

_____

_____

GENERAL RULE 4 (FORM 7: Small Group's Consensus on Rules and Procedures)

Procedures

1. _____

_____

_____

2. _____

_____

_____

3. _____

_____

_____

4. _____

_____

_____

5. _____

_____

_____

Procedures

1. _____

_____

_____

2. _____

_____

_____

3. _____

_____

_____

4. _____

_____

_____

5. _____

_____

_____

FORM 8— PROCEDURES

Procedures from Small Group to Total Group

Because the total group reached consensus on the rules on Form 4, this activity will develop accord on procedures for each of those rules. Under each rule, write all the procedures the small groups developed. Don't duplicate the procedures. If a procedure has already been mentioned, just put a check beside it to denote agreement.

GENERAL RULE **1** (FORM 8: Procedures from Small Group to Total Group)

Procedures

1.

2.

3.

4.

5

GENERAL RULE 2 (FORM 8: Procedures from Small Group to Total Group)

Procedures

1.

2.

3.

4.

5.

GENERAL RULE 3 (FORM 8: Procedures from Small Group to Total Group)

Procedures

1. _____

_____

_____

2. _____

_____

_____

3. _____

_____

_____

4. _____

_____

_____

5. _____

_____

_____

GENERAL RULE 4 (FORM 8: Procedures from Small Group to Total Group)

Procedures

1. _____

_____

_____

2. _____

_____

_____

3. _____

_____

_____

4. _____

_____

_____

5. _____

_____

_____

Procedures

1.

2.

3.

4.

5.

FORM 9—RULES & PROCEDURES

Final School Rules and Procedures

Taken from the entire group list, reach consensus and develop your final two to four procedures (practices) under each rule. This will be the final group project. You will have your school's rules and procedures after this is completed.

GENERAL RULE **1** (FORM 9: Final School Rules and Procedures)

Procedures

1.

2.

3.

4.

5.

GENERAL RULE 2 (FORM 9: Final School Rules and Procedures)

Procedures

1.

2.

3.

4.

5.

GENERAL RULE 3 (FORM 9: Final School Rules and Procedures)

Procedures

1.

2.

3.

4.

5.

GENERAL RULE 4 (FORM 9: Final School Rules and Procedures)

Procedures

1.

2.

3.

4.

5.

Procedures

1.

2.

3.

4.

5.

QUESTIONS AND ANSWERS ON RULES AND PROCEDURES FOR EDUCATORS

My work and travel around the country with schools interested in character education have resulted in some wonderful discussions on the role of rules and procedures in schools. Following are some questions and answers that were offered by educators concerning rules and procedures. I hope their concerns and responses will be helpful to you in your efforts.

Question...

By making a standard set of rules and procedures for all teachers in a school, I relinquish the authority that I have, as a teacher, to make an individual decision concerning the enforcement of a rule, the practice of a procedure or the implementation of a consequence. Is this a valid concern?

Answer...

This is a valid concern. Where does the authority of a teacher end and the need for consistency throughout a school begin? Various individuals have offered different slants on this issue. One primary teacher argued that it was impossible, and perhaps not desirable, for primary students to be completely quiet in the hall. She felt that requiring students to be silent in the hallway was wrong. Others in the group recognized her concern, but reminded her that students who talk loudly to other students in the hall disrupt others. Whispering can quickly become much louder and result in disruptions.

Secondly, some of the teachers felt that asking children not to talk in halls unless talked to by an adult was an important habit to develop in children as young as kindergartners. It may be difficult at first, but if all primary teachers are consistent, children can develop the habit of not talking in the hall—unless talked to by an adult.

If noise in the halls has not been a problem with teachers in the past in a school, then it should not be raised now. Rules are developed as expectations of appropriate student behavior. The rule is not needed if the students are already exhibiting good behavior. They already must know it or understand the expectations of civil behavior.

Question...
Getting highly structured in rules and procedures can interfere with what I value in the classroom. It doesn't bother me if students are a little late. If I haven't started class, then this is not a very big deal. Secondly, why should I feel that I should always agree with the school? These students are mine and I reserve the right of autonomy.

Answer...
What do we want our children to learn? Do we want them to learn to budget their time and be accountable for being punctual, or does it matter from teacher to teacher? Some may consider this a violation of the autonomy of the teacher, especially if the teacher teaches the same children all day with no other teachers involved.

However, this is not the norm. Even in elementary schools, students have multiple teachers. The need for consistency is crucial for helping students know what is expected of them in the regular classroom, as well as in P.E., art, music and other similar courses. This should not change from teacher to teacher. If so, it becomes too confusing for the students and results in loss of instructional time for the teacher.

Now, this does not mean that a teacher can't have some procedures or practices in the classroom that are different from those of other teachers. For instance, a teacher may want students to check math papers in a certain way, or have them turn their papers in after they have evaluated their own work according to a prescribed system. This is fine. However, all teachers must follow the rules and procedures that have been agreed upon by the others in the school, especially concerning basic civilities and students' movements in and around the school.

Question...
You feel that students can contribute to the establishment of rules and procedures. Isn't that the job of the teacher or the school?

Answer...
Students can contribute to the rules and procedures of a school. The establishment of rules and procedures is a job of teachers, but it is not theirs exclusively. Students know what contributes to a good environment. We hope they are committed to doing their part in creating a civil environment. Ask their input; they spend the day with you. Ultimately, it is the teacher's responsibility to insure a good, safe climate in the classroom, but students can help.

Question...
Character education seems to reflect the opposite of the self-esteem movement. Isn't it important that children feel good about themselves, and can't character education actually damage their self-esteem?

Answer...
It depends on how you define self-esteem. If you believe that it is based only on getting *my* needs met and *my* feelings respected, then character education or any climate that expects civility can hurt a child's self-esteem—by that definition. *Feeling* good is not the same thing as *being* good. Self-esteem is earned through accomplishments and the development of positive traits and attributes that are shared with others.

Developing good habits that contribute to social and/or academic success will enable students to feel good about themselves. Self-esteem must be earned. It cannot be given away like stickers on a primary student's paper. Developing positive self-esteem requires that students and adults interact with caring and trust. Self-development demands that one seek the guidance, care, discipline and love of others.

Bibliography

Adler, Ronald B. and George Rodman. *Understanding Human Communication*. New York: Rinehardt & Winston, 1982.

Bennett, William. *The Index of Leading Cultural Indicators: Facts and Figures on the State of American Society*. New York: Simon & Schuster, 1994.

Beck, Ken and Jim Clark. *The Andy Griffith Show Book*. New York: St. Martin's Press, 1985.

Damon, William. *Greater Expectations*. New York: Free Press, 1995.

Goleman, Daniel Goleman. *Emotional Intelligence*. New York: Bantam Books, 1995.

Gossen, Diane Chelsom. *Restitution: Restructuring Schools Discipline*. Chapel Hill, N.C.: New View Publishing, 1992.

Kelly, Richard. *The Andy Griffith Show*. Winston-Salem, N.C.: John F. Blair, Publisher, 1981.

Hester, Joe Bridges. *Building Relationships and Resolving Conflicts*. Chapel Hill, N.C.: New View Publishing, 1995.

Josephson Institute of Ethics. 1996 study of 6,000 high school students, Marina Del Rey, Calif.: Josephson Institute of Ethics Publishing, 1996.

Kauffman, James, and Harold Burbach. On creating a climate of classroom civility. *Phi Delta Kappan* 79, No. 4 (December 1997), pp. 320-325.

Kilpatrick, William. *Why Johnny Can't Tell Right From Wrong.* New York: Simon and Schuster, 1992.

Landers, Ann. *Winston-Salem Journal.* June 15, 1997.

Leming, James. In search of effective character education, *Educational Leadership* 51, No. 3, November 1993: 63-71.

Research and Development Center for Teacher Education at the University of Texas. *Organizing and Managing the Elementary School Classroom.* Austin, Texas: UT School of Education, 1981.

Scheve, Kristin. A Class Act: First graduates of Afrocentric program shine, *Winston-Salem Journal.* June 7, 1997.

Sweeney, Jim. *Tips for Improving School Climate.* Arlington, Virginia: American Association for School Administrators, 1988.

Wilson, James Q. *The Moral Sense.* New York: Free Press, 1993.

Wong, Harry and Rosemary Wong. *The First Days of School.* Sunnyvale, Calif.: Harry Wong Publications, 1991.

Wynne, Edward and Kevin Ryan. *Reclaiming Our Schools: A Handbook on Teaching Character, Academics, and Discipline.* New York: Merrill Press, 2nd ed., 1997.

About the Author

Dr. Philip Fitch Vincent brings more than 20 successful years of experience in education to his work. With an academic background in philosophy, religion, and psychology, Dr. Vincent received his master's degree in education from Appalachian State University in 1979 and his doctor of education degree in curriculum and instruction from North Carolina State University in 1991.

He has taught at the elementary, middle, and high school levels in North Carolina and Alaska, and has taught education courses at North Carolina State University. He has been a director of middle-grades education in North Carolina's Catawba County school system.

Dr. Vincent has authored or co-authored 18 books, including *Philosophy for Young Thinkers* and the best-selling books *Developing Character in Students—A Primer for Teachers, Parents & Communities*, and edited two volumes of *Promising Practices in Character Education—Success Stories from Across the Country*. Among journal articles he has written are articles about developing character, gifted education, computer ethics, and working with at-risk students in an alternative classroom setting. He is a regular contributor to various educational publications.

Dr. Vincent makes keynote presentations and conducts workshops with schools and parents on a variety of educational topics. He has been a featured speaker at many national education conferences including the following: Association for Supervision and Curriculum Development (ASCD), Virginia Superintendent's Conference, Kenan Ethics Program at Duke University, Georgia Dept of Education Service Learning Conference, North Carolina Principals' Executive Program, New Jersey Character Education Conference, N.C. Superintendent's Executive Program, St. Louis Personal Responsibility Education Process Conference, National School Board Association, Midwest Principals' Conference, Oregon Association of School Administrators, Florida Character Education Conference, Louisiana Department of Instruction, Florida Character Education Conference, South Carolina Character Education Conference, North Carolina Middle Schools Association, N.C. DARE Conference, Character Counts Coalition–Connecticut Conference, North Carolina Character Education Conference, Florida Thinking Skills conference. He has also lectured at Charleston Southern University, Olivet College, Western Carolina University, Georgia Humanities Council, and New Mexico School Administrators Association, among many others.

In North Carolina, Dr. Vincent has worked with more than 33 school districts in formulating and implementing their character education programs as well as schools and school districts in 23 other states.

Recognition that Dr. Vincent has received includes a teaching merit award, a grant from the Council for Basic Education, and Phi Kappa Phi and Phi Delta Kappa induction.

MORE GREAT RESOURCES

Title

Title	Quantity	Price	Total
ADVISOR/ADVISEE CHARACTER EDUCATION 24 Lessons to Develop Character in Students, SARAH SADLOW		$24.95	
GROWING CHARACTER DEB AUSTIN BROWN 99 Successful Strategies for the Elementary Classroom		$19.95	
TEACHING CHARACTER—IT'S ELEMENTARY 36 Weeks of Daily Lessons for Grades K–5, SADIE BROOME AND NANCY HENLEY		$27.95	
TEACHING CHARACTER IN THE MIDDLE GRADES 36 Weeks of Daily Lessons for Grades 6–8, BROOME, HENLEY,		$22.95	
DEVELOPING CHARACTER IN STUDENTS, 2nd Edition A Primer for Teachers, Parents & Communities, PHILIP VINCENT		$19.95	
BUILDING CHARACTER THRU SERVICE LEARNING Lessons From Eighteen Principals of the Year, DR. KATHY WININGS		$19.95	
READING FOR CHARACTER: 40 LESSONS for Middle Schools, based on The Book of Virtues, LINDA SHAIL		$19.95	
PARENTS, KIDS & CHARACTER 21 Strategies for Helping Your Children Develop Good Character, HELEN LEGETTE		$15.95	
DEVELOPING CHARACTER FOR CLASSROOM SUCCESS Strategies for Secondary Students, CHARLIE ABOURJILIE		$12.00	
RULES & PROCEDURES IN CHARACTER EDUCATION The First Step Toward School Civility, PHILIP VINCENT		$10.00	
RULES AND PROCEDURES VIDEO The First Step Toward School Civility, 44. MIN, PHILIP VINCENT		$59.95	
TEACHING CHARACTER Teacher's Idea Book, ANNE DOTSON & KAREN WISONT		$24.00	
Parent's Idea Book, ANNE DOTSON & KAREN WISONT		$12.00	

SHIPPING:
Up to $25 .... $4
$25 to $100 .... $6
Over $100 .... 6%

Subtotal	
NC Tax (6%)	
Shipping	
Total	

Form of payment: Check ☐ PO # _____

Make checks payable to:
Character Development Publishing, PO Box 9211, Chapel Hill, NC 27515-9211

Ship To:

Name _____

Organization _____ Title _____

Address _____

City: _____ State: _____ Zip: _____

Phone: (___) _____ Signature: _____

FAX ORDERS: (919) 967-2139

For further information, or to schedule a Character Development Workshop, call **(919) 967-2110**, or e-mail to **Respect96@aol.com** or visit our WebSite at **charactereducation.com** (Call for quantity discounts) R&P803

CHARACTER
DEVELOPMENT
G R O U P
PO Box 9211
Chapel Hill, NC 27515

CHARACTER DEVELOPMENT GROUP offers complete resources, including publications and staff development training for the planning, implementation and assessment of an effective character education program in schools and school systems.